GET LUCK NOW!

Bring Good Luck to Every Part of Your Life

BILL JAMES

BILL JAMES
For permission requests, write to the publisher, at william@getlucknow.com
www.getlucknow.com

Printed Worldwide
First Printing 2024
First Edition 2024

ISBN: 979-8-9913706-0-8 (Paperback)

Library of Congress Control Number: 2024917390

10 9 8 7 6 5 4 3 2 1

GET LUCK NOW!

Bring Good Luck To Every Part of Your Life

Table of Contents

Introduction

Welcome!

Greetings, fellow luckologists and aspiring luckologists!

Wait! Luckologist? That isn't a word!? This Bill James guy is already inventing crazy and strange terminology, and we are only two sentences into the book!

My dear reader, it is most definitely a word, and my goal for you is to also become a Certified Luckologist. This book will guide you along this path. I have read many books and spent years studying many ways to bring good luck into one's life. I have also attended seminars and training courses on luck and similar energy-type forces. Luck could happen in business, in health, in personal relationships, in finances, and in day-to-day life. Please keep an open mind and enjoy this book—I had a lot of fun putting it together and I plan for it to be an evergreen space to explore different ways to bring good luck into one's life.

The focus of this book is on GOOD luck. Seeking out and allowing for favorable outcomes in your life. So, when I say luck, I am almost always referring to good luck. That is the kind of luck that I want, and that I want for you, so that is my focus.

My definition of luck

Luck is an unseen force or energy that is always present with us. That is the good news. The more challenging news is that luck can sometimes be slightly elusive and sneaky in appearing to you. It can also be like a quantum effect—meaning luck doesn't necessarily appear unless one is looking for it or expecting it. This can work for good luck, which is what this book is focused on bringing into your life. But it can also work for bad luck. We won't talk much about bad luck because I assume that you do not want to bring that into your life. However, through our actions, thoughts, inactions, and other tricks of the mind, many people do, in fact, bring bad luck into their lives. Again, we won't talk much about that, but it is important to recognize that just as there are ways to bring GOOD luck into our lives, there are ways to bring the other kind of luck forward as well.

This luck force weaves through your everyday life in what would be considered mundane, boring moments, and it also can be with you in amazing, life-changing moments. Overall, it is available to you to use to your benefit, should you realize, understand, and choose to act on this knowledge. While some people are naturally tuned into luck and extract maximum value from it without really making a huge effort (or seemingly not making any effort!), the reality in life is that most people must actively cultivate the discovery of it in any given situation. The good news is that it is a skill and competency that can be developed by following the tips in this book!

Another way to think about luck is that it is an unseen force that can be used for your benefit that can be brought into existence through a series of actions and beliefs. Anyone who is reading this book can tap into the force of luck and use it to for themselves.

What I Believe About Luck

1. Luck is something everyone can tap into—both good luck, which most people want—but also bad luck, which (most) people don't want. We will focus on getting good luck into our lives.
2. I call the potential for luck that exists in a given situation Ambient Fortune™.
3. Ambient fortune is often paired with a universal invitation that leads us to the good luck.
4. Luck is available in unlimited quantities.
5. Luck can be a win-win situation. If you have great luck, I can also have great luck and so can your friends and family.
6. Luck can benefit finances, relationships, health, business, and everyday life.
7. Specific actions and being proactive can bring more good luck into your life.

Luckologist Qualifications

You may ask if I have had good luck in my life to qualify me to be writing about luck. I don't have a monopoly on the ideas of creating good luck, but I do believe I have several qualities that make me an aspiring luckologist who can help you on your journey. A few of these are below.

1. I believe myself to be a lucky person, so I am self-qualified.
   #I-gave-myself-a-certificate!
2. I am acting to actually create, write and distribute this book, and taking action is one way you can help bring luck into your life.
3. I have studied creating good luck and taken action to bring it into my life.
4. Being born in the United States to a caring family who provided me with love, a great education, a nice home to grow up in, healthy food, all kinds of sports activities, taught me to play chess, sent me to piano lessons, took cool vacations and trips and who were (and are!) very supportive of me all qualifies as very lucky.
5. I got into my dream college and graduated in four years with a degree in Finance.
6. I have been fortunate to have had a series of very interesting jobs in real estate, the investment management division of a trust company at a bank, and as an asset allocator and investor at top 10 endowment in institutional asset management.
7. I have traveled to six of the seven continents (still need to get to Africa!).

8. Twice in my life I skidded a car on ice and snow-covered roads. One time, it was a complete 360 turn at highway speeds, and the car ended up just gently coasting into the middle of the highway median and there were no damages to the car or injuries to myself, my passenger or anyone else who driving on the highway. Another time, on an icy road (no snow!), I spun the car 180, crossed the center lane, and ended up backwards on the other side of the road's shoulder, right between two telephone poles. I guess this could be considered bad luck that these scary situations happened, but I considered it good luck that nothing major happened. Both events happened decades ago, and since then I took an ice and snow driving class, which honestly wasn't geared as much toward safety, as it was towards learning how to move quickly on the snow and ice. But, since these events, I have a great respect for snow- and ice-covered roads, so go pretty slow most of the time and have stayed safe.

9. I went skydiving over 30 years ago and landed successfully. Some people probably think I landed on my head, but I did not. It was with two instructors at once holding onto the sides of my skydiving rig while we dropped in a formation until I pulled the chute open at the designated height. We had to climb out on a little rail outside the plane before we let go as we all got situated. I experienced everything just like a solo skydiver would including being in charge of steering the parachute when it opened and landing by myself. It was not a tandem jump, but something called

accelerated freefall. It was extremely scary, and I am still here! I have not done another jump.

All these things seem like good luck to me, and as you will see, I feel beliefs are a very strong part of one's reality. The fact that I believe this brings it into my reality, and tells me that yes, I am lucky.

And really, whether you think I'm qualified or not, I would ask you to keep forging ahead and reading through this guidebook. I think you will find many nuggets of wisdom you can use to bring good luck into your life.

To finish the introduction, I ask you to reflect for a moment on what things in your life qualify as good luck events. Maybe getting a date with someone, and marrying that person? Or getting a dream job, starting your own company, or getting into the school of your dreams? Maybe having kids or grandkids? Maybe you haven't had a major 'lucky' event by your definition, but I would ask you to look around and see your house or apartment, or maybe you're in a coffee shop reading this, or reading it on your smartphone. I would say you have a start on being considered a lucky person just by the fact that you are having any of those experiences! Remember to believe and expect good luck in your life. Now, you can't JUST believe your way into good luck, you need to help it along and let the universe know that you are ready for good luck to enter into your life. This book will help you to do that.

How This Book Is Organized

I love books that summarize each section. I can quickly breeze through these books, get the key knowledge, and dig in further if I need to. This book will be organized that way.

Framework of Get Luck Now!

- Each chapter will begin with a list of key points
- The text will discuss those points
- Most chapters finish with Lucktivities, which are actions to take now to get luck*

*A note on the Lucktivities—I have used a couple different formats for them throughout the book, and if you have one you like more let me know for the print version of the book and I may make all of them consistent! For now, there are some that are paragraphs describing the Lucktivity, and others are comprised of detailed step by step instructions.

Summary of the Book

- <u>Believe</u> good luck is something you can bring into your life.
- <u>Keep an open mind</u> about what happens to you in life, and always ask yourself "What is great about this?"

- Learn to discover the Ambient Fortune™ in each situation (defined in Chapter 2)
- Look for underline universal invitations to bring you to the good luck that is available.
- Try lots of things—food, meeting new people, talking to people, business ventures, books, music, events, learning opportunities, travel destinations, physical activities. The more things you try, the luckier you will be.
- Network with people as frequently as possible.
- Do something nice for another person every day if you can with no expectation of payment or being owed something back.
- Accept that good luck is a journey. There will be wins and challenges. Without contrasts, life would be boring.

I greatly appreciate your interest in this book and thank you for reading it! Enjoy yourself!

Bill James, CL*
Granger, Indiana
August 31, 2024

P.S. If you have suggestions or anecdotes about things you've done to bring good luck into your life, please share these ideas with me at william@getlucknow.com I'm happy to receive feedback about the book. It is my first book ever, and while I'm proud of that I also recognize I can make a lot of improvements. I focused on getting it written and having lots of actionable content! Thank you!

*Certified Luckologist—see Lucktivity on page 21 to give yourself a title!

Chapter 1

Your Mindset Activates Luck

Key Points

- Your mindset is the foundation to create your own luck
- Ask yourself the right questions to support that mindset
- Recognize the power of belief and expectations to attract luck

Everything you do starts with a belief. Your beliefs can contribute to your life in positive ways, or they can hold you back and limit what you do. Therefore, working as hard as possible to have a positive mindset is the foundation of all that is to come in the Get Luck Now! process. Beginning by acknowledging the importance of beliefs and working to keep positive self-talk high and negative thoughts to a minimum will set you up for success.

In 1993, a friend and I attended an Anthony Robbins seminar in Chicago. It was called Unlimited Power. During that 3-day seminar, we walked across hot coals on the first evening of the event! We told ourselves the mantra "cool moss, cool moss, cool moss" as we walked across the coals. I'm sure there's a scientific explanation for why most people don't get burns on their feet doing this. I mention Anthony Robbins because he is a highly successful author and peak performance coach. His writings and exercises have helped me greatly through the years. He believes that the quality of a person's questions helps to determine the quality of their life. People with better lives ask better questions. I think that is a powerful and accurate way to view the world. Regarding the mindset of luck, there are questions one can ask themselves constantly to install a luck-attracting mindset. Some of these questions are in the tips below.

In addition to questions, expectations and beliefs are a key part of attracting luck into your life. Every day, if you look for and expect greatness and excellence in yourself and others, you will likely see it, because you are focusing on it. Even if you don't get all the way to greatness and excellence, it is much better to be priming yourself this way instead of starting off looking for the worst in the world. It is easy to get down and focus on the negative, but focusing on excellence and greatness is the way to good luck. Believe that all of this is possible, and you can be right.

Lucktivities

Lucktivity: Luck Visualization Exercise

The Luck Visualization Exercise is a daily mental practice designed to reinforce your identity as a lucky person and prime your mind to recognize and attract fortunate opportunities. By vividly imagining yourself experiencing luck, you're training your subconscious to be more attuned to lucky situations in real life.

Detailed Steps

1. Prepare

Find a quiet, comfortable space where you won't be disturbed for at least 10 minutes. Sit or lie in a relaxed position. Take a few deep breaths to center yourself and clear your mind.

2. Set the Scene

Close your eyes and imagine yourself in a neutral environment (e.g., a white room or a peaceful garden). Visualize a soft, golden light surrounding you. This light represents luck and positive energy.

3. Visualizing Lucky Scenarios

Imagine a series of lucky events unfolding in your mind's eye. These can be: Realistic everyday occurrences (e.g., finding a parking spot right in front of your destination); Major life events (e.g., landing your dream job) Fantastical scenarios (e.g., winning the lottery).

For each scenario, engage all your senses: What do you see happening? What sounds do you hear? Can you feel any physical sensations? Are there any smells or tastes associated with the experience?

4. Emotional Engagement

As you visualize each lucky scenario, allow yourself to feel the positive emotions associated with it: Joy, Excitement, Gratitude, Confidence. Really immerse yourself in these feelings, letting them fill your entire body.

5. Affirmations

As you experience these lucky scenarios, mentally repeat affirmations such as: "I am a magnet for good fortune," "Lucky opportunities find me easily," "I am always in the right place at the right time."

6. Transition

Slowly bring your awareness back to your physical surroundings. Take a few deep breaths, feeling relaxed and positive. Open your eyes, carrying the feeling of being lucky with you into your day.

Sample Visualization Sequence

Imagine yourself walking down a street and finding a $100 bill on the sidewalk.

See the green of the bill catching your eye. Feel the excitement as you bend to pick it up.

Hear yourself saying, "Wow, what a lucky find!"

Visualize receiving an unexpected call offering you your dream job.

Hear the phone ringing and the voice on the other end. Feel your heart racing with excitement. See yourself pumping your fist in celebration.

Imagine running into an old friend who connects you with an amazing opportunity.

See their familiar face in an unexpected place. Feel the warmth of their hug. Hear them saying, "I have something perfect for you!"

Tips for Success

- Practice consistently: Aim to do this visualization exercise daily, preferably at the same time each day.
- Start small: Begin with 5-minute sessions and gradually increase to 10-15 minutes.
- Be vivid: The more detailed and multi-sensory your visualizations, the more impactful they'll be.
- Stay positive: If negative thoughts intrude, gently redirect your focus to the lucky scenarios.
- Blend reality and fantasy: Include both realistic and fantastical lucky scenarios to cover all bases.
- Update regularly: Refresh your visualized scenarios to keep the exercise engaging and aligned with your current goals.

Advanced Practice

As you become more comfortable with the basic visualization, try these ideas:

- Create a "Luck Vision Board" with images representing your visualized lucky scenarios.
- Record a guided visualization for yourself to use during the exercise.
- Practice "micro-visualizations" throughout the day, quickly imagining lucky moments.
- Combine visualization with physical actions (e.g., visualize luck while holding a "lucky" object).

Keep a "Luck Visualization Journal" where you record:

The scenarios you visualized.

How you felt during and after the exercise.

Any lucky events that occur in your real life that mirror your visualizations.

By consistently practicing this Luck Visualization Exercise, you're programming your mind to be more receptive to lucky opportunities. You're also building a stronger self-image as a fortunate person, which can boost your confidence and positivity, further attracting good luck into your life.

Lucktivity: Ask Great Questions

- Frequently ask yourself these questions to get into a good luck mindset:
- Why do great things always happen to me?
- What cool things are going to happen today?
- Who are the amazing people I'm going to meet soon?
- What interesting fact or story does this person have to share with me today?
- How can I help each person I interact with today?

What cool thing am I going to hear and learn in this meeting / call / event right now?

Comment: Your mind will come up with answers to these questions, whether or not you have an answer at the exact moment. So roll with it, ask yourself the questions, and see how much luck you generate! Also, think about this the next time you're tempted to ask yourself a question that may not be so positive. For example, if your dishwasher breaks, do NOT ask yourself "Why do things like this always happen to me?" because your brain will find an answer, and it may not be so helpful to you. Instead, in this kind of situation, ask yourself "What is right or great about this?" Maybe it will be as simple as "Well, I get a new dishwasher since the old one gave out. The new one is quiet, uses less energy, and looks cool." This is the mindset you want to install.

Lucktivity: Create positive stereotypes.

The following technique I learned from the book Quantum Jumps by Cynthia Sue Larson: Create positive, proactive stereotypes for anything you are doing. For example, I would say to myself, "Lots of people just like me who write books on finding good luck have amazing success with it. It happens all the time!" Telling yourself that it is no big deal—this event happens all the time—allows your mind and brain to process things in a positive way for you. Bringing good luck to you!

Further Discussion of This Idea

This Lucktivity involves consciously creating and reinforcing positive stereotypes about yourself and your circumstances to attract more luck and success. By repeatedly telling yourself that certain positive outcomes are common and expected for people like you, you're programming your subconscious to look for and create these outcomes in your life.

Detailed Steps

1. Identify Areas for Positive Stereotyping

List aspects of your life where you'd like to see more luck or success. Include personal characteristics, skills, and circumstances.

2. Craft Positive Stereotype Statements

For each area, create a statement that frames success as common for "people like you." Use present tense and make the statements feel natural and believable.

3. Personalize Your Statements

Adjust the wording to feel authentic to you. Ensure the statements resonate with your personal experiences and aspirations.

4. Create a Daily Affirmation Routine

Choose a consistent time each day to repeat your positive stereotype statements. Consider morning and evening as powerful times for this practice.

5. Visualize the Stereotypes in Action

As you say each statement, vividly imagine yourself embodying that positive stereotype. Engage all your senses in this visualization.

6. Look for Evidence

Throughout your day, actively seek out evidence that supports your positive stereotypes. Celebrate when you notice alignments between your statements and reality.

7. Refine and Expand

Regularly review and adjust your statements based on your experiences. Add new positive stereotypes as you grow, and your goals evolve.

Examples of Positive Stereotype Statements

"People with my background often find great success in this industry."

"Individuals who approach challenges like I do frequently stumble upon innovative solutions."

"Those who share my values typically attract supportive and influential mentors."

"People with my skill set naturally gravitate towards lucrative opportunities."

"Folks from my hometown have a knack for thriving in new environments."

Tips for Success

- Be Consistent: Repeat your statements daily to reinforce the new mental patterns.
- Stay Realistic: While positive, your stereotypes should still feel believable to you.
- Be Flexible: Allow your stereotypes to evolve as you grow and your circumstances change.
- Share Selectively: Choose carefully who you share this practice with to avoid negative feedback, but constructive feedback can be helpful!
- Combine with Action: Use these stereotypes as motivation to take steps aligned with your goals.

Potential Pitfalls and How to Avoid Them

Overreliance on stereotypes without action. Solution: Use stereotypes as motivation for proactive behavior.

Creating unrealistic or grandiose stereotypes. Solution: Start with modest, achievable stereotypes and gradually expand.

Feeling inauthentic or experiencing imposter syndrome.
Solution: Ground your stereotypes in your genuine strengths and experiences.

Reflection Questions

After practicing this technique for a while, ask yourself:

1. How has my perception of myself and my possibilities changed?
2. What new opportunities or lucky breaks have I noticed since adopting these positive stereotypes?
3. How have these stereotypes influenced my actions and decisions?
4. In what ways can I expand or refine my positive stereotypes to align with my evolving goals?

Remember, the power of this technique lies in its ability to reshape your subconscious expectations and perceptions. By consistently reinforcing these positive stereotypes, you're training your mind to be more attuned to fortunate opportunities and to create the conditions for luck and success in your life.

Lucktivity: Avoid video-based news.

Avoid video-based news if you can. News is often negative and can affect your luck-attracting mindset. You can read newspapers, magazines, and other text-based sources. And if you can't eliminate video-based news, try a news diet of a few days to see how you feel. You won't miss anything, and you'll feel great. If you don't like it, then you can easily go back to watching as much news as you want. You will like it if you try it.

Lucktivity: Make up Your Own Title / Qualification.

You notice in the introduction of this guidebook that I called myself a Certified Luckologist. Of course, until I called myself this, there wasn't any such title out there. But if you think about all the titles or certificates that are out there, a lot of them are just made up. Someone had to create the title in the first place. Why not create your own title for something that you want to model in yourself? For example, if you wanted to start being a better gardener, you could call yourself "The Guru of The Garden." If you were in a long line at the Chik-fil-A drive-through, maybe all of a sudden you become the "Duke of the Drive-through." Now yes, this is totally ridiculous, but you can have fun with it and reinforce what you're trying to learn/do/become. Another example could be if you're working out and wanting to get into better shape like pretty much everyone always is—call yourself the Commander of the Gym. You can see where I'm going with this. Endless possibilities. Fun. Ridiculous. Always remember that good luck can be fun and ridiculous. You probably won't be putting these titles on LinkedIn, though you never know!

My inspiration for this was the knighthoods given out by the United Kingdom and having a history in England long before the UK even existed. The source of the honor is the head of state. I mean sure, they have a bunch of history on their side, blah blah blah, but it was originally just some person (king) giving a knighthood out to someone because they wanted to honor them. Well, we are each our own heads of state, in charge of ourselves, right? So why not just give yourself a title anytime you want that meshes with something you want to bring into your life!

The fact is, whether we actually give ourselves a named title, we are always playing a role of some kind in our lives. The role of a parent, of a caregiver, of a worker, etc. etc. While playing these roles, we probably almost never assign ourselves a title to fulfill those roles, except maybe in our jobs. That doesn't mean you can't give yourself a title, though! You have the power to give yourself any title you want!

The Concept

This Lucktivity involves creating a unique title or qualification for yourself that embodies your aspirations, skills, or the lucky persona you want to cultivate. By playfully "certifying" yourself, you're reinforcing a positive self-image, setting intentions, and potentially opening doors to new opportunities.

Detailed Steps

1. Identify your Focus area

Reflect on an area of your life where you want to attract more luck or success. Consider skills you're developing, qualities you admire, or goals you're pursuing.

1. Brainstorm Creative Titles

Let your imagination run wild - be playful and don't self-censor. Combine words in unexpected ways to create unique titles.

2. Refine Your Title

Choose a title that resonates with you and feels empowering and ensure it is memorable and potentially conversation starting.

3. Create a Mock Certification

Design a fun, unofficial "certificate" for your new title. Include your name, the title, and a brief description of what it represents.

4. Embody Your New Title

Act "as if" you truly hold this qualification. Consider how someone with this title would approach situations in your focus area.

5. Share Selectively

Introduce your title in appropriate social settings as a conversation starter. Be prepared to explain the concept with humor and self-awareness.

6. Evolve Your Title

As you grow and your goals change, allow your title to evolve. Create new titles for different areas of your life as needed

Examples of Creative Titles

- "Contessa of Culinary Competence" as you prepare dinner or lunch.
- "Certified Luckologist"—what you will be after finishing this book.
- "Senior Sanitation Specialist" as you clean the house or take out the trash.
- "Doctor of Optimistic Outcomes"—for bringing yourself great luck!

- "Professional Test Taker"—maybe if you're in college or working on passing a certification for a job for, say, nursing for example.
- "Duke of the Drive-Through" when getting your dinner or lunch and waiting.
- "Maestro of Mondays" as you get ready for a Monday workday.
- "Princess of Piano Practic" as you learn the piano and practice scales. Yay!

Words to Help You Come Up with a Title

Duke/Duchess, Diva, Deity, Certified, Registered, Qualified, Master, Commander, Precept, Captain, Adjudicator, Leader, Chartered, Technician. What words would you use in your title and add to this list?

Tips for Success

- Keep it lighthearted: This exercise should be fun and playful, not too serious.
- Be confident: Embrace your title with a mix of humor and genuine belief.
- Align with goals: Choose titles that reinforce your actual aspirations and efforts.
- Use as motivation: Let your title inspire you to take actions aligned with its meaning.
- Be flexible: Don't be afraid to change or create new titles as you grow.

Potential Pitfalls and How to Avoid Them

Taking title too seriously/literally. Solution: Maintain balance of playfulness & genuine intention.

Feeling like an imposter. Solution: Remember that the title is a tool for growth, not a claim of expertise.

Negative reactions from others. Solution: Be selective about when and with whom you share your title.

Reflection Questions

After creating and embodying your title for a while, ask yourself:

1. How has this title influenced my mindset and actions?
2. What new opportunities or lucky breaks have I encountered since adopting this title?
3. How has my self-perception changed?
4. In what ways can I more fully embody the qualities represented by my title?

Advanced Practice

- Create a "Board of Directors" for your life with various titles for different aspects.
- Develop a backstory for your title, including how you "earned" it.
- Use your title as a framework for setting and achieving goals in its related area.

Remember, the power of this technique lies in its ability to shift your mindset and reinforce positive self-image. By playfully adopting a unique title, you're giving yourself permission to embody the qualities and attract the opportunities associated with it. This can lead to increased confidence, creative problem-solving, and potentially lucky breaks as you approach life with this new, empowered perspective.

BILL JAMES

Chapter 2

Ambient Fortune™

Key Points:

- In any given situation in life, there exists the potential for great fortune
- This is called Ambient Fortune™, and it is always present
- You can tap into Ambient Fortune to have more good luck and success in life

Ambient Fortune™ is a term I developed to describe the potential for good luck to occur, and this potential exists in any given situation. That's why ambient is part of the phrase. Ambient literally means 'all around,' like when someone says 'ambient temperature' it is the temperature all around us. Or ambient noise—it is the noise that is all around us, the background noise. Ambient, in the context of ambient fortune, means that there is a potential fortune of good luck always around us, waiting to be released or discovered by each of us. The potential is always there for good fortune and opportunity to be revealed to us. If you can tune into this, if you can be aware that this fortune is there, waiting for you, you can realize the full potential of the moment. Therefore, it is an ambient fortune™ present in each and every moment of your life! And yes, I did get a trademark on this!

Interesting side note on trademarking a phrase—in the United States, you must go through the U.S. Patent and Trademark Office. It is a straightforward process that can be done online and with or without the assistance of an attorney. I used an attorney to help me just to be sure I did everything right, but it was still easy. The U.S Patent and Trademark office is backed up for many months. There is a wait time of almost eight months before a trademark is reviewed by their lawyers. Usually, the whole process takes around a year to complete. The main reason given for the extremely long wait times is a combination of a huge number of filings on wordmarks and phrases, as well as a general shortage of examiners (lawyers) at the patent office. Maybe AI will help speed up the wait times in the future, but for now there is a huge wait.

Ambient Fortune is an interesting concept because it is compatible with many of the leading theories of how the world works underneath what we see and observe. For example, the "many worlds theory" of how things work basically states that every time we make a decision, we are branching off ourselves into different timelines—some of whom become successful and happy, and some of whom don't quite get the same levels of success. Ambient Fortune theory is compatible with this because if you 'discover' the fortune hidden in each situation (or said differently, if you take yourself onto your favorable timeline), you will branch yourself off into the positive world where all your dreams and wishes are happening. You can do this many times and have an amazing life!

Ambient Fortune is also compatible with the "virtual universe / simulation theory," which basically states that we are in a simulation that is so complex that it ultimately doesn't really matter because the way the simulation is constructed is beyond our understanding. However, even if that is true, Ambient Fortune can still come into play because a virtual reality or simulation has the capability to become anything at any time, and Ambient Fortune therefore can come into existence at any time because of this. Again, this can lead you to a favorable outcome. You have found the 'fortune' in your particular circumstance.

To tap into Ambient Fortune, we need to cultivate awareness, openness, and mindfulness. These qualities can help you to tune into the possibilities of good luck that exist at any moment in time. The challenge for many successful people is that they are remarkably busy. They have very full calendars—business meetings, family activities, social events, volunteering, etc. There is always another meeting to go to or a task to complete. It can be difficult to stay grounded and aware of ourselves and our surroundings in the current moment. Of course, the current moment is all we ever have, so the more we can be aware of this and understand what is happening from moment-to-moment, the more likely we will be able see and welcome luck into our lives.

Have you ever noticed a situation that is 'inviting' you to do something? This is something to be on the lookout for, and that can help you access the fortune part of ambient fortune. I call these 'universal invitations,' meaning that the universe is inviting you in some way to notice and act on something that will likely bring good luck to you. An example universal invitation from my life, a long time ago, happened in Las Vegas. I was taking a seminar called The Do's and Don'ts of Dice, from a gentleman named Michael Vernon, aka 'the professor.' Michael is an expert in what he calls applied metaphysics. While on the surface this seminar was about the game of craps and winning at craps, he really uses the craps tables of Las Vegas as his laboratory to show what is possible with his applied metaphysics teachings. Because outcomes occur rapidly in craps—the rolls of the dice—if one is reading the energy and playing effectively, you will know right away if your approach is aligned with how the dice are rolling. In other words, if you are winning, you're probably aligned with the energy and good luck that is there—the ambient fortune using my term.

So what happened at the seminar that caused me to say this was a universal invitation? Well, one night we were at the Rio playing craps, and the table we found ourselves at was low-energy and not much was happening. We would win a little, then lose, win a little, and back and forth like this for maybe 30 minutes. Then a loud group of about seven guys entered the casino and walked towards the craps tables. At that precise moment, a new craps table was opened up, and all these guys went to that table. Michael Vernon immediately said, "That's our invitation to go where the energy is and play at the newly opened table." Turns out, the guys were there for a bachelor party, and were playing craps before going on to some clubs later. Well, it definitely was an invitation for us to play, because we all won a bunch of money and had a really fun time! Of course it is easy to say in hindsight that this invitation was easily spotted, but we could have just as easily told ourselves that 'oh man do we really want to be playing next to these loud obnoxious people." Again, mindset and expectations come into play here!

Michael Vernon chalks this up to being in tune with the energy of the table, the people, and his experience. But I'm sure you can think of a time in your life when someone said, "let's do X, Y or Z" and you decided to do it even though maybe at the time, you didn't think it would be that great. But then you surprised yourself you had a great time! There are opportunities like that around us all the time if we just stay open to them and aware of ourselves and the energy and environment, and the invitations that may be making themselves known to us. In Chapter 4 I have an excellent example of saying 'yes' to an invitation that led to a great experience.

Other examples of universal invitations could be a friend inviting you to an event, seeing an ad for an interesting seminar or course online, reading about a unique travel destination after you had been thinking about going somewhere, or other things that come into your life that might be slightly unexpected. If you keep an open mind you may see these universal invitations more clearly and easily!

Being prepared to find the good luck from Ambient Fortune involves 4 things:

1. Keep an open mind and cultivate a sense of curiosity about life and experiences.
2. Constantly be on the lookout for 'universal invitations' to accept, that will help you find the Ambient Fortune in a situation.

3. Be flexible, adaptive, and resilient when on your journey of life.
4. Trust your intuition and act when opportunities present themselves.

I fall into the camp of someone who has a checklist for everything. I like everything to be set up so I can try to ensure myself of the perfect experience, whether that is eating at a restaurant, driving somewhere far, or any number of things in my life. I am constantly working on being more 'in-the-moment' and letting myself go with the flow, but it is tough for me! But by starting with the idea of awareness of the moment and tuning into the little invitations that the universe may be sending to you, you can bring great luck into your life!

Ambient fortune is such a powerful concept and I'm still discovering unique aspects to it and working out ways to harness it and apply it to one's life.

I would like to write a follow-up book to this one that solely focuses on ambient fortune so I will keep you apprised!

Lucktivities

Lucktivity: Luck Journal

Keeping a daily luck journal can help train your mind to notice and appreciate lucky occurrences, reinforcing a positive mindset. Here's a suggested format:

1. Get a dedicated notebook or use a digital app for your luck journal.
2. Each day, write down at least one lucky thing that happened, no matter how small.

3. Include the date and a brief description of the lucky event.
4. Optional: Rate your overall feeling of luckiness for the day on a scale of 1-10.
5. At the end of each week or month, review your entries to see patterns or growth in your luck awareness.

You could also get an ornate leather-bound book to do this to emphasize the mystery and excitement that can accompany good luck. Or whatever format speaks to you, of course!

Lucktivity: Luck Ritual

Many people have a morning or evening ritual, where they prepare for the day or reflect on what just happened. If that's you, try to work this tip into your routine. Ask yourself these questions during that time, or really anytime during the day: "What lucky situations will I find myself in today?" "In what ways will this person / meeting / call bring luck into my life?" I ask myself these questions throughout the day, and at this point it is a habit to always be excited about what lucky things may happen. Try this—it will work if you keep at it! You will be focused on lucky things happening in your life and see them happen.

Lucktivity: Gym Equipment

This is a tip for the gym. Especially during crowded times but it could also apply at other times with regards to a popular piece of equipment. For example, if the leg press machine is always occupied, ask yourself "I wonder in what way this leg press machine is going to be available to me at the exact time I need it today?" This will put you in the frame of mind to be aware of the machine, when it may be available, and also you may just find yourself near it and someone may just be finishing up.

Lucktivity: Waiting in Line

This tip applies to waiting in line and works best when there are multiple queues in place like at a supermarket. It may not be that effective in a single line queue, which scientifically is usually the quickest kind of line anyway. So how do you do this one? Quickly scan the lines you have to choose from, and when you see one that looks the shortest to you, just pick it. Then, if you can, have patience and be 'in the moment' observing if your line goes faster than the others. If it does go fast, great! If not—even better! Unless there is a major delay, it won't be a big deal, and you can smile to yourself either way. Did this tip bring you luck? Kind of? I think good luck is often about how you react to the world, and that you get what you want to focus on.

I also apply this one to the toll booths when driving. Now, maybe (and hopefully) toll booths will be a thing of the past with overhead and open road tolling becoming more common, but as of now I go through the Chicago Skyway tolls fairly often and have an I-Pass so can usually breeze through pretty quickly. But every so often, someone in front of you has an issue with their pass, and it causes a small delay. If I'm the one behind this person, I always take that opportunity to take a deep breath, and make a little game by saying, okay I think this will take...umm 2 minutes to resolve. That way I'm not upset or worried about a little delay. I also will try to tidy up the car a little bit, but usually when I think about all that stuff the person is on their way. All good!

Lucktivity: Surface Area of Luck

Increase your surface area of luck. This concept was originally conceived by a computer programmer named Jason Roberts. He stated that a person's chances of getting lucky are defined by the following equation: Luck = Passionate Doing x Effectively Telling What You're Working on. So you can increase your chances of having good luck by doing something you are passionate about and telling that effectively to as many people as possible. This makes a lot of sense and also takes into account the effects of a large network increasing someone's chances of having good luck. You can also ask yourself before deciding to do something (or not!) the following question: What action will increase my surface area of luck? An example would be deciding to go to the networking session after your conference even though you are tired and would rather chill out by the pool by yourself, but if you went to the networking session you obviously have a much greater chance to meet someone who can help you or that you can help with something they are working on.

By embracing the concept of Ambient Fortune and practicing these lucktivities, you can increase your awareness of the lucky opportunities that surround you every day and learn to capitalize on them to bring more fortune into your life.

Do you have any examples of Ambient Fortune that you've experienced in your life? How about a unique universal invitation that you answered to great success? I would love to hear any interesting or amazing examples if you'd like to share them! william@getlucknow.com

Chapter 3

Big Networks = Big Luck

Key Points

- The bigger your network, the luckier you will be
- More people who know what you're working on, allows for that one perfect person(s) to be in position to help you
- Learning more networking strategies will increase your luck potential
- Personal and virtual networks are valuable

Your network is made up of personal connections (friends, family, and acquaintances) and business connections (customers, colleagues, co-workers, vendors, contractors, people in your industry, etc.). The more connections you have, the luckier you will be. Why? The more people that know about you, and what you are doing—whether in business or in your everyday life—the more likely that one of those many people will be able to help you with what you are working on. Also, the more likely that YOU will be able to help someone else out with something. Bringing good luck into your life is a multi-directional process. Good luck is unlimited, and the more you can help others get good luck, the more good luck there will be in the world overall. This will eventually find its way back to you.

I wish I were better at networking. I feel like I could be a lot better if I just reached out to a few people every week via email or calling. Usually, people are pleasantly surprised and pleased to hear from me (and I'm sure you) especially if you're just calling or reaching out to catch up and not sell something. But, if you are selling something or working on something, most people will be happy to hear about it as long as you are sharing it in an authentic and friendly way.

I read an article a few years ago titled "The Rise of the Solo Capitalists," by Nikhil Basu Trivedi of the firm Footwork.VC. This article discussed venture capital firms that were run by one person only. The article made the point that these firms are all about the brand of the individual running them, and that this personal brand was the key to the success of the firm/person. Many of these solo capitalists are influencers on X, LinkedIn, or YouTube. Many are former founders and have had successful exits by selling their businesses. Their massive networks, made up of founders and tech-savvy individuals, gravitate to them because of their insights, knowledge, and presence on social media and as well as in other networking spaces. They created their own networks, and they nurture these networks by posting, providing valuable content, and engaging with their followers and friends, and they get business deals coming to them and opportunities they otherwise wouldn't see if not for their networks.

I can also see this in podcasts. People I know that have interesting podcasts are effectively making extensions of themselves to go out into the world 24/7 and make the case for themselves to people they don't even know! This is the ultimate networking flex! I'm sure this brings them into contact with people they never even knew existed, but that are eager to talk to them and share a business opportunity or to network or just become friends. You can also say this about YouTube videos and other evergreen kinds of content. Content creators who are able to attract fascinating guests, while being good at asking questions and making the guests feel comfortable and getting them to open up are really successful with this approach.

We are all super busy, I get that. Making time to network and reach out to others, especially when we don't have a specific need can take a lot of effort. It is worth it! People are almost always happy to hear from their friends even if it is a quick text or email or post on a social media site. By doing this consistently, you will nurture your network and have it help generate good luck for you in unexpected ways! I have neglected social media as a networking tool for a long time and I'm working on changing that! So, feel free to call me out on this if you see I haven't posted more frequently on LinkedIn and X!

Lucktivities

Lucktivity: Weekly Connection Challenge

Look across your LinkedIn, Facebook, X, or another social networking platform at your connections there. Make it a point to reach out to at least two people each week that you haven't contacted in a while. Ask them how they're doing, maybe share what you're working on.

Lucktivity: Lucky Introduction

Each week, try to introduce two people in your network who you think could benefit from getting to know each other. This creates goodwill and expands your influence. Eventually, it could be difficult because you've connected everyone. That would be a cool situation to be in!

Lucktivity: Podcast / Speaking

Go on someone's podcast or start a podcast! I have to admit this one scares me; I have never done it even though I have a good friend who has asked me to do a podcast for many years! As the host. I guess I am afraid I'd say something stupid and then it would be out there in eternity for someone to listen to and laugh at. That fear certainly doesn't stop a lot of people from doing podcasts, and yes there are some ridiculous things out there, but this is a such a strong tip for increasing your luck. I have seen it be phenomenally successful for lots of people (← positive stereotype alert!). Maybe someday…

Lucktivity: Talking with Everyone in Your Day-to-Day Activities

As you go about your day, make it a point to say hi to the waiter or waitress, cashier, or store attendant and ask them, genuinely, how they are doing.

Really, this applies to all people you come into contact with during the day. Of course you need to do your errands, etc. so it will depend on how much time you have whether you can talk to everyone especially if you're hurrying around! You could compliment them on their customer service or just tell them you appreciate them being there. I was at the gym the other day, and as I was leaving, I noticed the guy walking near me had a t-shirt with a picture of a glider on it and "New Zealand" written on it. As we were both walking to the parking lot, I said "Hey have you been to New Zealand?" And he stopped to chat and told me he was there about 10 years ago and took a glider ride over parts of the South Island. It was a really interesting story and having been to New Zealand myself a long time ago, I generally knew the area he was talking about. This was a nice interaction that was easily started. Multiply that out over the course of a year that by just noticing something (a t-shirt logo) you could have an interesting story to tell and learn something cool.

Chapter 4

Luck Grooves to Your Moves

Key Points

- Luck favors those who take action
- Overcome fear and hesitation when pursuing opportunities
- Develop a proactive approach to creating your own lucky breaks

As you sit on your couch binge-watching your favorite series, revel in amazement as luck easily flows towards you. You are in the right place, right now. NOT!

Luck is best generated through movement, activity, and action! To attract luck into your life requires you to act and be on the offensive. Showing up at an event. Making a phone call. Emailing someone. Asking for the sale. Writing that book. You need to take action to get luck. The more actions you take, the more likely good luck is to come into your life. Luck can be a flywheel that keeps bringing more and more luck to you and it all starts with actions.

I can relate to the lack of taking action. This book has been something I've been thinking about for a long time. Many years. I have been reading about luck, taking seminars, and trying to put into practice many of the things in this book. Except the part about taking action and writing! Someone finally convinced me that it would be a good idea to make this book, and that people would be interested in it. This simple vote of confidence was enough to compel me to write the book, and for that I am thankful. People have already reached out and said they are excited to be reading this book and that they look forward to it! Now, based on my beliefs that people want to help me, I do genuinely believe that. My hesitation is still there, and I fear that people may criticize me and laugh at my efforts, but I'm writing it anyway and my stronger belief is that many people will like it, and it will have a very positive effect on many people's lives! And also, I worry that this won't really be considered a book since it isn't very long, but hey, I'm going to consider it a book!

I mentioned in Chapter 1 that I'd share a story relating to accepting an invitation and taking action. It happened a little over 10 years ago. A co-worker of mine had invited me to dinner for a Thai meal. He and his wife had spent time in Thailand in their early post-college years and they learned how to make some delicious dishes while there. They had also just had a baby so wanted to introduce me to their new family member. Well, I had been doing a lot of traveling for work and was feeling tired, so I asked if we could take a raincheck on the dinner. My coworker insisted I come over, telling me that his wife had been working all day making an outstanding Thai dinner, and they really wanted me to meet the new baby. He was very persuasive. Other than being tired, I really didn't have a reason to say no, so I said sure I'll come by. The dinner also happened to taking place very near my birthday, which will become important in one second. When I arrived at my coworker's house, he opened the door with the new baby in his arms, and I of course marveled at the cute baby in that instant. Then, he threw the door wide open and SURPRISE! Several of my coworkers were yelling 'Surprise' and 'Happy Birthday' all at the same time. They really got me! Everyone had parked out of sight of the street, so I didn't suspect anything when walking to the front door of their house. It was the only time anyone has ever surprised me with a party like this. I was very moved and grateful they would do this for me. Now this was pretty much all my co-worker and his wife's doing, but by taking action and just showing up, I had an amazing experience, and it also allowed everyone else to have the experience of surprising someone with a party! What's the quote that 95% of life is just showing up? I tend to agree with this the longer I live!

Another story I have regarding taking action involves the recent solar eclipse that took place in April 2024. I was originally going to go watch it in Ohio with some friends of mine but at the last second decided to go to Indianapolis because I thought the weather forecast looked slightly better. So, I was going by myself, which was no problem! When I got to the White River State Park on the day of the eclipse, there were a ton of people all excitedly waiting for the start. I was walking around and saw many intricate telescopes and camera setups trying to catch the totality. One group of people had an interesting device aimed at the sun called a Seestar which was basically a high-res camera, solar filter, and tracking computer-in-one, that streamed a picture of the sun to a smartphone. I took the opportunity to strike up a conversation with the group, and it turned out they had seen many different eclipses over the years. I asked if I could watch the eclipse with their group and they said "Yes, definitely!" I had made a cereal box with the pinhole in it, and surprisingly that also got a lot of attention from people but wasn't nearly as cool as this group's Seestar device. I had a great time watching the eclipse with them, and basically all I had to do was say hi and ask if I could watch with them. Taking action!

These might sound like minor things, but my entire point is that almost every cool experience involves YOU being proactive and doing something to move yourself into the good parts of the ambient fortune that exist in a given situation but may at first be hidden from sight. To tap into that fortune, you must first put yourself in the situation where it exists!

A final thought I will leave you with regarding taking action. Think about all the knowledge we have access to in our lives, instantaneously from the internet and the library. We know how to eat well and exercise to be in great shape. We have many books and guides on starting a business, investing successfully, having great friendships and relationships, and traveling to interesting places. In other words, everyone knows (or can quickly learn) how to do all these things. What separates the ultra-achieving people who actually are in shape, super successful in business, have lots of friends, and have great lives? These people have TAKEN ACTION to make these things happen for themselves, using that knowledge. Consistently eating well. Consistently working out. Making things happen by starting a business. Networking with people. Are these things easy? No. Are they simple? Yes. I'm pointing all this out because everyone who has been successful, with rare exceptions, has achieved their success by continuously taking actions in their lives to make it happen.

Lucktivities

Lucktivity: Take Action Right Now!

Take action to do something—that class you've been meaning to take, getting a book read that has been sitting on your table, reaching out to a friend you've lost touch with. Simply taking a small action can lead to a snowball of luck getting bigger and bigger! Go ahead and take action right now!

The Concept

This Lucktivity is all about overcoming inertia and procrastination to create momentum in your life. By taking immediate action on things you've been putting off, you open yourself up to new opportunities and potential lucky breaks.

Detailed Steps

1. Identify Delayed Actions

Make a list of things you've been meaning to do but haven't gotten around to yet. Include both small tasks (like reading a book) and larger goals (like taking a class).

2. Prioritize Your List

Rank the items on your list based on potential impact and ease of accomplishment. Choose one item to act on immediately.

3. Set a Timer

Commit to spending just 15 minutes on your chosen task right now. Use a timer, maybe the one on your phone, to make this commitment concrete.

4. Take Immediate Action

Start working on your chosen task as soon as the timer begins. Focus solely on this task for the full 15 minutes.

5. Reflect and Plan

After the 15 minutes, reflect on what you accomplished and how you feel. Decide whether to continue working on this task or schedule another 15-minute session.

6. Create an Action Habit

Commit to doing this exercise daily for a week. Each day, choose a new task from your list or continue progress on a larger goal.

7. Track Your Progress

Keep a "Take Action" journal to record what you work on each day. Note any positive outcomes or lucky breaks that result from your actions. This can be part of your luck journal if you created one already. You could make this a section of your luck journal if you started one.

Examples of Actions to Take

- Read the first chapter of a book that's been sitting on your table.
- Send a message to reconnect with an old friend.
- Research and sign up for a class you've been interested in
- Clean out a cluttered drawer or closet.
- Start writing the first draft of a project you've been thinking about

Tips for Success

- Start small: Choose actions that feel manageable to build momentum.
- Celebrate every action: Recognize that taking any action is a win, regardless of the outcome.
- Be consistent: Try to take action at the same time each day to build a habit.
- Stay open to opportunities: Pay attention to any new connections or ideas that arise from your actions.
- Share your commitment: Tell a friend about your "Take Action" practice for accountability.
- Sometimes if I have a task I'm not super excited about (doing laundry, vacuuming, etc.) I might do a 15-minute burst or even a 5-minute burst just

focused on that activity, and you will surprise yourself with how much you can get done!

Reflection Questions

After each action session, ask yourself:

1. What did I accomplish in this short time?
2. How do I feel after taking action?
3. Did this action lead to any new ideas or opportunities?
4. What's the next action I can take to build on this momentum?
5. Were there universal invitations the I noticed while taking these actions?

Remember, the goal of this Lucktivity is not just to complete tasks, but to create a proactive mindset that attracts luck and opportunity. By consistently taking action, you're signaling to yourself and the universe that you're ready and open to receive good fortune.

Lucktivity: Become a Yes Man or Woman

One idea I've seen written about says that you should become a yes man or woman. What do I mean by this? Say yes to everything that comes your way. A party invite? Yes. Someone wants to go to a movie you really don't think will be that great? Yes. Trying a new food? Yes. This can get you out of your comfort zone, and at the same time, get you into new situations and experiences that may be exactly where the ambient fortune is waiting for you! In recent years I seem to have read more about trying to say no to things in order to free up your schedule, but by saying yes to things you may pleasantly surprise yourself. I admit, I'm not the greatest at this myself, though I am trying to be more of a yes man!

The Concept

This Lucktivity challenges you to open yourself up to new experiences by saying "yes" to opportunities that come your way. By doing so, you increase your exposure to potential lucky breaks and tap into the ambient fortune that surrounds you.

Detailed Steps

1. Set Your Intention

Commit to a specific timeframe for your "Yes" challenge (e.g., one week, one month).

Write down your intention and why you're doing this challenge.

2. Define Your Boundaries

Establish clear guidelines for what kinds of invitations you'll say yes to.

Ensure your "yeses" are safe, ethical, and within your means.

3. Create a "Yes" Tracker

Use a journal or app to log each invitation you receive and your response. Note the date, the invitation, your initial reaction, and the outcome.

4. Practice Mindful Acceptance

When an invitation comes, pause before automatically saying no. Take a deep breath and consider how this might be a universal invitation.

5. Say "Yes" and Follow Through

Commit fully to the experience once you've said yes. Approach each new situation with curiosity and openness.

6. Reflect on Each Experience

After each "yes" adventure, journal about what you learned or gained. Look for unexpected benefits or connections that arose.

7. Adjust and Extend

Review your experiences weekly and adjust your approach as needed.

Consider extending your "Yes" challenge if you're seeing positive results.

Examples of Things to Say Yes To

Invitations to social events, even if they're outside your usual circle.

Opportunities to try new foods or restaurants.

Requests to help with projects or volunteer work.

Invitations to participate in new activities or sports.

Chances to learn new skills or attend workshops.

Tips for Success

- Start small: Begin with low stakes "yeses" to build your comfort level.
- Stay safe: Prioritize wellbeing and don't say yes to anything dangerous or illegal.
- Be authentic: Your "yes" should come from a place of genuine openness, not obligation.
- Embrace discomfort: Remember that growth often happens outside your comfort zone.
- Balance your energy: It's okay to space out your "yeses" to avoid overwhelm.

Reflection Questions

After each "yes" experience, ask yourself:

1. What did I learn from this experience?
2. Did I meet any interesting people or discover any new opportunities?
3. How did this experience challenge or change my perspective?
4. What unexpected benefits came from saying yes?

5. Was there a universal invitation that I answered to make this happen?

Potential Pitfalls and How to Avoid Them

Overcommitment. Solution: Set a daily or weekly limit on the number of "yeses."

Neglecting self-care. Solution: Include "yes" options that involve rest and rejuvenation.

Feeling inauthentic. Solution: Regularly check in and adjust your challenge as needed.

Remember, the goal of becoming a "Yes Person" is not to abandon all discretion, but to open yourself up to more of life's possibilities. By saying yes more often, you're creating more opportunities for luck to find you and for ambient fortune to manifest in your life.

Lucktivity: Embrace the No

This is a very scary one for me! Setting a goal to receive a certain number of "no's" each month can be a powerful way to overcome fear of rejection, increase your actions, and potentially lead to unexpected lucky outcomes. I was inspired to include this after reading the book by Jia Jiang called "Rejection Proof." Read his book for some great stories on him getting rejected and accepted.

The Concept

The idea behind "Embrace the No" is to reframe rejection as a positive step towards success. By actively seeking out situations where you might be rejected, you:

1. Reduce fear of rejection through repeated exposure to it.
2. Increase your number of attempts, thereby increasing your chances of success. You will eventually find someone that says 'yes' to even a crazy request!
3. Build resilience and confidence.
4. Open yourself up to unexpected opportunities.

Detailed Steps

1. Set your "No" Goal

Start with a manageable number, like 5 "no's" per month. Gradually increase this number as you become more comfortable.

2. Create a "No" Tracker.

Use a spreadsheet, app, or notebook to track your "no's". Include columns for: Date,

Action Taken, Result, Lessons Learned.

3. Identify Potential "No" Situations

Asking for a discount at a store where they really never allow discounts.

Pitching an idea to your boss or asking for a massive raise.

Asking someone out on a date.

Applying for a job you think might be a stretch.

Requesting an informational interview with someone you admire.

4. Take Action

Commit to pursuing these situations, focusing on the act of asking rather than the outcome.

5. Celebrate Your "No's"

Treat each "no" as a victory – it means you took action! Realize it is just a response and nothing personal directed towards you. Reflect on what you learned from each experience.

6. Look for Hidden Opportunities

Sometimes a "no" can lead to unexpected alternatives or connections.

You could put this in your luck journal and use the below as a sample entry:

Date: August 20, 2024

Action Taken: Asked for a 10% discount at local electronics store.

Result: No discount given.

Lesson Learned: Learned about price-matching policy, which could be useful in the future.

Unexpected Outcome: Salesperson mentioned an upcoming sale next week.

Tips for Success

- Remember that "no" often just means "not right now" or "not in this exact way."
- Focus on quantity over quality initially – the goal is to take more action.
- Be respectful and gracious when receiving a "no."
- Look for patterns in your "no's" to identify areas for improvement.
- Celebrate your courage in asking, regardless of the outcome.

By embracing "no's", you're not only increasing your chances of eventually getting "yes's", but you're also opening yourself up to a world of unexpected opportunities and building the resilience that's crucial for attracting luck into your life. Again, to me this is scary, so it probably means there is something really profound about this exercise!

Lucktivity: Daily Micro-Adventure

The concept of a daily micro-adventure is about doing one small thing each day that's outside your normal routine. This practice can open you up to new experiences, perspectives, and potential lucky encounters.

Micro-adventures are designed to break you out of your comfort zone in small, manageable ways. They increase your exposure to new people, ideas, and opportunities, and can help you to cultivate a mindset of curiosity and openness. They also create more chances for serendipitous encounters. More chances to see a universal invitation leading to ambient fortune!

Detailed Steps

1. Commit to having one micro-adventure today. It doesn't have to be big or time-consuming - small changes count!
2. Brainstorm Ideas—Create a list of potential micro-adventures to draw from when you need inspiration. Include a mix of social, culinary, cultural, and physical activities
3. Act—Follow through on your micro-adventure, even if it is uncomfortable.

Reflect and Record—At the end of each day, jot down what you did and any interesting outcomes. Consider keeping a "Micro-Adventure Journal" to track your experiences. This could also be part of your luck journal.

Example Daily Micro-Adventures

1. Culinary Adventures: Try a new cuisine or restaurant. Cook a dish you've never made before. Sample an exotic fruit or vegetable from the grocery store.
2. Social Micro-Adventures: Strike up a conversation with a stranger (e.g., in line at the coffee shop). Attend a local meetup or event you wouldn't normally go to. Reach out to an old friend or acquaintance you haven't spoken to in a while
3. Route Shake-Ups: Take a different route to work or while running errands. Explore a new neighborhood in your city. Get off at a different bus or subway stop and walk the rest of the way
4. Learning Micro-Adventures: Learn and use an unfamiliar word each day. Watch a short documentary on a topic you know nothing about. Try a free online class in a subject outside your usual interests.
5. Physical Micro-Adventures: Take a short walk during your lunch break in a new direction. Try a new type of exercise or workout. Do a quick 5-minute stretch or yoga routine at an unusual time of day.
6. Creative Micro-Adventures: Doodle or sketch something during a break. Write a haiku about your day. Take a photo of something beautiful or interesting you spot during your day.

Tips for Success

- Start small - even tiny changes to your routine count.
- Be open to unexpected outcomes.
- Don't judge the adventure by its immediate results - sometimes the benefits are not immediately apparent.
- Mix it up - try to vary the types of micro-adventures you have.
- Be present and mindful during your micro-adventures to fully experience them.

Lucktivity: Spontaneity Day

Designate one day a month as "Spontaneity Day" to open yourself up to new experiences and potential lucky opportunities. Here's how you might structure this:

1. Choose a specific day each month (e.g., the first Saturday).
2. Commit to saying "yes" to any safe and legal opportunity that presents itself.
3. Prepare yourself mentally the night before, reminding yourself to be open to whatever comes your way.
4. At the end of the day, reflect on your experiences and any unexpected positive outcomes.

You could also write down on a few pieces of paper a few out-of-the-ordinary things for you to do, throw them into a box or hat and draw one at random and commit to doing that item today. Of course, this wouldn't be totally spontaneous, but it would have an element of uncertainty and excitement to it. A stretch here would be to have a trusted friend or family member write down the spontaneous things that you needed to do; hence it would be truly spontaneous, for you! Maybe this would be a fun weekend activity for the whole family or with a group of close friends.

Another stretch idea for the Spontaneity Day would be to designate a day to explore the area near your house, say in a 25- or 50-mile radius.

You would randomly pick a direction to drive whatever distance you set, and wherever you ended up you would explore that area. You could set the idea of 'restaurant' or 'park' or 'unique shop' as a target place for you to explore once you got 25 or 50 miles away.

Chapter 5

Embrace the Journey of Luck

Key Points

- Recognize that luck is a lifelong journey of growth and discovery
- Enjoy the process of creating your own luck and celebrate your successes
- Develop a long-term perspective on luck and refine strategies over time
- Contrasts in life are what allow us to recognize the good times and make life fun
- Setbacks and failures are part of the journey to luck
- Develop strategies to bounce back from adversity and maintain a positive outlook
- Learn from your experiences and adapt your approach as needed

I like to frequently remind myself that everyone is on a journey in life. This journey will have highs and lows; everything won't always be perfect with never-ending luck raining down on you. You will have notable milestones—graduating from college, your first job, romance, maybe having kids, traveling, making great friends, losing friends and family, and many other highs and lows. Good luck can be an essential element of your life, if you choose to embrace it and look for it. Understand that it is always hanging around, waiting to be grasped by you, even when it looks like you are in a challenging situation.

We've explored quite a few tips and techniques for creating your own luck and discovering it in hidden places. Many readers probably already have their own luck rituals and practices that they are using for themselves. The process of using what you know now, and learning new techniques to complement your existing knowledge, is a smart approach to keep getting better and better at being aware of luck.

To appreciate the good times in our lives, we do need to experience a full breadth of emotions and trials. If we didn't have challenges and hard times, how would we fully understand how nice the great times in our lives are? These contrasts keep life exciting and interesting. It might be pretty boring if everything was perfect, and you were always basking in good luck—though maybe someday I'll let you know if I reach this state.

Roger Federer gave a commencement address where he told the graduates that over the course of his career, he won 54% of all the points he played. Roger is considered possibly the best tennis player of all time. So in other words, if you view each point of a tennis game as a win/loss, Roger lost 46% of the time. If you thought about your own life, and things you've tried, and if you had a record of winning 54% of the time and losing 46% of the time, you might consider that a big failure. I know I generally would! We come from a hyper competitive world where anything less than a 100% is often considered a failure. Roger Federer's statistics can make it clear that there is another path—one that embraces losses or setbacks as part of your journey to success. Of course, life does not come with the simple set of rules that tennis does, and 'keeping score' like this is pretty much impossible to do. But having said that, if you view your wins and losses in the context of a journey that you are on, and that on that journey there will be temporary wins and temporary setbacks, you can better equip yourself to bounce back and welcome luck into your life when it appears to you. I note that the top sports gambling services also have win/loss rates around 53% wins 47% losses.

Here's a story of embracing the journey of luck that happened to me a couple months ago. I took a drive to Florida to visit my dad and stepmom. It is a long trip—1,130 miles one-way! On the return trip there was an area of road construction in Kentucky, and I hit some kind of hidden crack or hole in the highway with my front passenger side tire while going over 60mph. There was a huge BANG sound, and I thought for sure I was going to have my tire blow out. I checked it at my next safe opportunity to take a break, and amazingly there was nothing really to see. I figured I got a lucky break with the situation!

Well, fast forward about a month, and by that time I had driven another few hundred miles in my car. I was running some errands and realized I had forgotten my phone—which is rare—so I thought maybe it fell behind the car seat. I went around to the passenger side and opened the door and was crouching down trying to see if the phone was under the seat. While I was doing that, my eyes were close to the front tire, and I noticed what looked like a small balloon pressing from the inside of the tire out. There was also about a one-inch rip with some unusual white fibers and rubber material poking out of the rip. It didn't look good, so I immediately drove to the tire shop about 5 minutes away. They said I was lucky I made it as my tires were run-flat and it seemed this one was about ready to give it up due to the damage in the ripped part of the tire.

I actually felt pretty lucky after all this. Why? A few reasons. 1) I safely drove my car for hundreds of miles after what was likely the initial damage a few weeks before. 2) I didn't blow the tire out, causing more damage to my car and 3) I avoided hurting myself or anyone else if this situation had caused an accident. While I wasn't too excited about the cost, I still felt very lucky about the tire. This story has a few points— bad luck from hitting the crack / pothole, then good luck to have had run-flat tires that prevented me from having a major problem right away, to good luck for being able to safely drive hundreds of miles after this happened, and then a small amount of bad luck forgetting my phone at home (no big deal!), but followed by great luck that I saw the status of the tire while looking for my phone. Again, to me, this was mildly annoying, but I really did feel lucky to have been given the opportunity to remedy the situation easily.

One other musing on embracing the journey of luck: When I was in middle school, I enjoyed the Choose Your Own Adventure series of books, where one would 'choose' their own way at critical points in the books. If the book was about a group of adventurers seeking treasure in some distant land, there might be a choice to climb a mountain path or continue into a valley below. Some decisions led you to a path of riches and success and some ended, let's say, rather abruptly! It wasn't always clear which choice would be best based on the way the author presented the alternatives. I used to spend a lot of time trying all the different paths in the book, and sometimes it was tough to actually exhaust all the choices without just paging through the book to see what I may have missed. I often think that life is kind of like these stories, except in life the choices aren't presented to us in a clear, multiple choice, either/or format. And that is the exciting thing—both the journey and the basically unlimited choices we have. We can choose to be fearful or worried about that fact, or we can embrace it, and enjoy the journey! I choose to embrace it!

Lucktivities

Lucktivity: Fortune Reframe

The Fortune Reframe is a daily exercise designed to help you perceive Ambient Fortune even in seemingly negative or challenging situations. By actively reframing events, you train your mind to spot potential universal invitations and lucky opportunities, even in challenging situations.

Detailed Steps

1. Event Selection

At the end of each day or week, reflect on events that occurred. Choose an event that you initially perceived as negative or challenging. Start with smaller annoyances and gradually work up to more significant challenges as you become more practiced.

2. Initial Reflection

Write down the event in detail. Note your initial emotional reaction and thoughts.

3. Reframing

Ask yourself: "How could this event be a universal invitation or a manifestation of Ambient Fortune?" Challenge yourself to come up with at least three possible positive outcomes or lessons. Consider both immediate and long-term potential benefits.

4. Opportunity Identification

For each positive reframe, identify a specific action you could take to leverage this potential opportunity.

5. Gratitude Practice

Express gratitude for the learning opportunity this event has provided. Acknowledge the potential for growth and positive change.

6. Follow-up

In a week's time, revisit this reframed event. Reflect on any positive developments or insights that have occurred as a result.

Example Fortune Reframe

Event: "I missed an important work deadline."

Initial Reaction: Stressed, disappointed in myself, worried about consequences.

Reframes

1. This could be an invitation to improve my time management skills. Action: Research and implement a new productivity system.
2. This might be pushing me towards having an important conversation with my boss about workload. Action: Schedule a meeting to discuss current projects and priorities.
3. This could be an opportunity to demonstrate my problem-solving skills in crisis management. Action: Develop a plan to mitigate the impact and prevent future occurrences.

Gratitude: I'm grateful for a chance to reassess work habits and communication strategies.

Follow-up: A week later, I've implemented a new project management tool and had a productive discussion with my boss about workload balancing.

Tips for Success

- Be patient with yourself. Reframing takes practice and may feel unnatural at first.
- Stay open to unexpected interpretations. Sometimes the most valuable reframes aren't immediately obvious.
- Don't force positivity. The goal is to find potential, not to deny the challenge of the situation.
- Share reframes with a trusted friend or family member for additional perspectives.
- Keep a "Reframe Journal" to track your progress and revisit past reframes for inspiration. You could have this as part of your luck journal if you want.

Advanced Practice

As you become more adept at the Fortune Reframe Practice, challenge yourself to:

- Reframe events in real-time, not just at the end of the day.
- Look for patterns to identify recurring themes or areas for personal growth.
- Apply the reframing technique to larger life events or long-standing challenges.
- Help others reframe their negative experiences, spreading the practice of seeking Ambient Fortune.

By consistently practicing the Fortune Reframe, you'll develop a habit of looking for hidden opportunities in every situation. This mindset shift can significantly increase your ability to recognize and capitalize on the Ambient Fortune that surrounds you daily.

For more ideas on reframing, Scott Adams has authored a great book called *Reframe Your Brain: The User Interface for Happiness and Success* that I highly recommend.

Lucktivity: What is right or great about this?

If you have a particularly challenging situation, ask yourself "What is right or great about this?" And if it is truly hard to come up with anything, ask "What COULD be right or great about this?" Even if you don't come up with an answer in the moment, your brain and mind will be working on this and likely come back to you with something positive out of the situation.

The Concept

This Lucktivity involves actively seeking out the positive aspects of any situation, especially those that initially seem negative or challenging. By asking "What is right or great about this?", you're training your mind to find opportunities for growth, learning, or unexpected benefits in every circumstance.

Detailed Steps

1. Identify the Situation

Choose a current challenge or seemingly negative situation in your life. If you can't think of one, start with a minor inconvenience in your day.

2. Pause and Breathe

Center yourself before reacting. Take three deep breaths to create mental space.

3. Ask the Key Question

Sincerely ask yourself: "What is right or great about this?" If nothing comes to mind immediately, add: "What COULD be right or great about this?"

4. List Positive Aspects

Write down at least three positive aspects or potential benefits of the situation. Push yourself to find more, even if they seem small or unlikely.

5. Explore Deeper Implications

For each positive aspect, ask: "How could this lead to something even better?" Consider both short-term and long-term potential benefits.

6. Identify Action Steps

Based on your positive answers, what actions can you take to leverage these benefits? Choose at least one action step to implement.

7. Reflect and Reinforce

At the end of each day, review situations where you applied this technique. Celebrate the shift in perspective and any positive outcomes.

Tips for Success

- Practice Regularly: Apply this technique to small situations daily to build the habit
- Be Genuine: Aim for authentic positivity, not forced optimism
- Start Small: Begin with minor inconveniences before tackling major challenges
- Stay Open: Sometimes the benefits may not be immediately apparent - remain open to possibilities
- Share the Technique: Encourage friends or colleagues to join you in this practice

Potential Pitfalls and How to Avoid Them

Toxic positivity or denying real problems. Solution: Acknowledge the challenge while looking for opportunities within it.

Using the technique to avoid taking necessary action. Solution: Use the questions as a springboard for constructive action, not avoidance.

Struggling to find positives in incredibly difficult situations. Solution: Start with "What COULD be right about this?" to open up possibilities.

Reflection Questions

After practicing this technique for a while, ask yourself these questions:

1. How has my overall outlook on challenges changed?
2. What unexpected opportunities have I discovered through this practice?
3. How has this reframing technique affected my stress levels and problem-solving abilities?
4. In what ways has this practice influenced my luck or perception of luck?

Advanced Practices

Revisit Past Events: Apply this technique to past challenges to uncover hidden benefits

Collaborative Questioning: Practice this technique in a group setting to gather diverse perspectives on challenges you may have experienced.

Anticipatory Questioning: Before entering a potentially challenging situation, preemptively ask, "What could be great about this?"

Luck Journal: Keep a journal of how this questioning practice leads to lucky breaks or positive outcomes.

Remember, the power of this technique lies in its ability to shift your perspective and uncover hidden opportunities. By consistently asking "What is right or great about this?", you're training your mind to see the potential for luck and positive outcomes in every situation, thereby increasing your chances of recognizing and capitalizing on fortunate circumstances.

Lucktivity: Annoyance to Opportunity

Look for hidden good luck that may be lurking in annoying situations. Think about the tire-being-damaged story I just shared. I could have gotten mad that I needed to get my tire fixed and that it was going to take time away from other things I wanted to do, but instead I focused on the fact that I was glad I had the chance to fix it before it got really bad and something or someone got damaged. Keeping a book or two in your car in case you ever have to wait somewhere is also a good strategy to use so you can be more productive with your time reading something you were going to get to anyway.

Lucktivity: Waiting to Enjoying

Turn a wait into an opportunity. Keep a book or notebook or something you may be working on in the car with you, so it is handy if you have a wait on your hands. For example, if you are at the doctor's office, you can usually have a wait. Bringing a book you're reading can make the wait go faster. It was something you were going to do anyway. I always see folks endlessly scrolling their phones while waiting, and while I also do that, I feel like the wait goes faster when I have a book handy or something more tangible to be working on. This can be a nice tool in your toolkit of lucktivities that makes a wait seem more like an exciting opportunity vs. something you don't look forward to.

The Concept

This Lucktivity involves transforming typically unproductive waiting times into opportunities for personal growth, productivity, or enjoyment. By being prepared for these moments, you can turn potential frustration into chances for luck and positive experiences.

Implementation Steps

Detailed Steps

1. Create a "Wait Kit"

Choose a small bag or container that's easy to carry. Fill it with items you enjoy or that help you be productive (e.g., books, notebook, puzzle book).

2. Identify Common Wait Scenarios

List situations where you often find yourself waiting (e.g., doctor's office, commute, queues). Perhaps make note the average duration of these waits.

3. Match Activities to Wait Times

For short waits (5-15 minutes): Quick puzzles, article reading, mindfulness exercises.

For medium waits (15-30 minutes): Book chapters, journaling, language learning apps.

For long waits (30+ minutes): Online courses, substantial reading, creative writing.

4. Prepare Digital Resources

Download e-books, podcasts, or educational apps on your phone. Organize into playlists or folders for easy access.

5. Set Wait Time Goals

Decide on specific goals for your wait times (e.g., read one chapter, learn five unfamiliar words). Track your progress to make the experience more rewarding.

6. Practice Mindful Transitions

When entering a wait situation, take a deep breath and consciously shift your mindset. View the wait as a gift of time rather than an inconvenience.

7. Engage in "Wait Networking"

If appropriate, use wait times to strike up conversations with others. Be open to unexpected connections or opportunities that may arise. This can sometimes be a unique challenge as often most people are engrossed in their phone screens while waiting. Usually, it is the entire waiting room!

8. Examples of Wait Time Activities

Read a book or e-book, listen to an educational podcast, practice a language with an app.

Work on a personal project (writing, planning, brainstorming), Do puzzles or brain teasers. Meditate or practice mindfulness, Catch up on correspondence (emails, messages, cards).

Tips for Success

- Always Be Prepared: Keep your "Wait Kit" stocked and easily accessible.
- Vary Your Activities: Rotate items in your kit to keep things fresh and exciting.
- Quality Matters: Choose activities you genuinely enjoy or find valuable.
- Stay Flexible: Be ready to engage in conversation if an opportunity arises.
- Celebrate Progress: Acknowledge what you accomplish during wait times.

Potential Pitfalls and Solutions

- *Forgetting your "Wait Kit".* Solution: Keep a backup set of activities on your phone

- *Feeling pressured to always be productive.* Solution: Include enjoyable activities in kit
- *Missing out on social opportunities.* Solution: Be open to interactions

Reflection Questions

After practicing this technique for a while, ask yourself:

1. How has my perception of waiting changed?
2. What unexpected benefits or opportunities have arisen during wait times?
3. How has this practice affected my overall productivity or personal growth?
4. In what ways has transforming wait times influenced my luck or perception of luck?

Advanced Practices

Wait Time Challenges: Set monthly goals for what you want to achieve during wait times

Luck Journal: Record any lucky encounters or ideas that come during these transformed wait times.

Skill Development: Focus on developing a specific skill using only your wait times.

Creative Output: Use wait times to work on a creative project (e.g., writing a book, learning to draw).

Remember, by transforming waiting time into enjoyable or productive moments, you're not just making better use of your time — you're also creating more opportunities for luck to find you. Whether through chance encounters, sudden inspirations, or the cumulative effect of consistent personal growth, this practice can significantly enhance your "luck surface area."

Concluding Thoughts

Thank you for reading Get Luck Now! I appreciate and respect you and hope that—through these pages and writing—you can feel me sending good-luck energy to you! It was fun putting together. I have a profound respect and deep appreciation for the authors who's work I leaned on and who did most of the research and discovering these ideas way before I ever did. You can read about many of these books in the annotated bibliography that follows.

I welcome the opportunity to hear from anyone who wants to reach out. I can be contacted at william@getlucknow.com and would especially be interested if you have unique ways you've brought good luck into your life, or if there is a technique I haven't mentioned you find particularly helpful that you would like to share. I'm also interested in learning about luck-related books, authors, Youtubers, Twitter/X people, interesting seminars or courses, and other types of content. If you'd be so kind as to share, I would be grateful. I fully recognize that my bibliography is not the final word on luck-related literature and guidance!

I would love to know your favorite Lucktivity that you try, and how you might add your own touch to make it special to you. Any ideas, please let me know, I'm excited to hear!

I hope to have a follow-up book, or maybe an extension of this book, which lists contributions from readers on techniques and tips that work for them. This would be an amazing thing to share and keep adding to over time! It may be an evergreen type of PDF or e-book that gets updated as ideas are added. I may dedicate an entire book to talking about ambient fortune™ since I believe that is such a profound concept. I am also interested in exploring universal invitations in their various forms.

I'm offering to make 2 free in-person speeches to discuss this book to the first two different people or groups who ask. If it is within a 2-hour drive of South Bend IN I will do the speech free, and if it is further than that we can talk about reimbursement for the trip costs. I will not take a fee for these speeches! These must be in-person and not Zoom or video based.

I also offer to be on anyone's podcast who reaches out, to discuss luck and Get Luck Now! I am also happy to discuss life in general on a podcast. This will be good for 3 podcasts.

One final thought...taking inspiration from Michael Vernon of Playing for Keeps, as well as Joseph Gallenberger, author of Inner Vegas, I have contemplated having an in-person seminar in Las Vegas to explore the concepts of ambient fortune in an environment where one could see the results of being 'tuned in' to the situation pretty quickly. If anyone would be interested in doing an in-person seminar sometime there (or another location), let me know. I feel like an in-person event could be a really cool experience and get some amazing feedback and insights in a group setting.

Wishing you good luck today and always!

Appendix 1
Annotated Bibliography

I would encourage interested readers to explore this bibliography of books and articles relating to luck and bringing good things into your lives. All these books contain pearls of wisdom that I've tried to distill into this book, and there are many more insights from these authors. Please note, I've written comments by many of the books, but not for all of them in case you are looking for comments on every book!

Adams, Scott. *Reframe Your Brain: The User Interface for Happiness and Success.* Scott Adams, Inc., 2023. Best known for creating the office-based comic strip Dilbert, Scott Adams has reinvented himself over time to be a political commentator and streaming star of his own making—the 'simultaneous sip' with Scott Adams nearly every day on the social platform scottadams.locals.com. He's written extensively about corporate culture and being successful in life. This book contains a huge list of ways to think about the world. Scott views things through a Usual Frame / Reframe model. Some of his examples are:

<u>Usual Frame:</u> <u>Reframe:</u>

Success depends on who you know. Success depends on how many people you know.

Your critics are evil monsters. Your critics are your mascots.

The universe is acting against you. The universe owes you.

Luck is random & can't be managed. You can go where there is more luck (energy).

Scott Adams is one of the most visible and vocal examples of a person who has a strong luck mindset. He also believes one can influence the universe to bring things into existence. Now you might say he is making an attribution error: he has had a lot of success in life, and he is attributing this to his 'ability' to influence the universe through willpower, influence, etc. Maybe that's true...but maybe he's onto something and is one of the few super-successful people openly talking about this stuff.

Aaronson, Deborah and Kwan, Kevin. *Luck: The Essential Guide.* The Society for Fortuitous Events, 2008.

Brault, Edouard. *Billionaire of Light.* Independently Published, 2023. Billionaire of Light talks about heightened states of consciousness, inner peace, more joy, and unconditional love. Mr. Brault considers himself to be an energy coach and has courses and much more information at his website edourardbrault.com. He also teaches courses on Udemy. You can find videos on his YouTube channel. This book leans heavily to the spiritual side of life, and while not precisely about luck, many of the concepts carry over. A unique person who embodies a luck-mindset!

Busch, Christian. *The Serendipity Mindset: The Art and Science of Creating Good Luck.* Riverhead Books, 2020.

Christensen, Clayton M. *Competing Against Luck: The Story of Innovation and Customer Choice.* Harper Business, 2016. Examines luck from a business perspective, and how businesses can use specific techniques to drive product innovation. The core tenet is the theory that consumers hire and fire products on the basis of 'Jobs to Be Done', and if you can view all products and services through this lens, it will help you to make better innovations.

Cohen, Ben. *The Hot Hand: The Mystery and Science of Streaks.* Mariner Books, 2021.

Gallenberger, Joe. *Inner Vegas—Creating Miracles, Abundance & Health.* Rainbow Ridge Books, 2013.

Dr. Gallenberger has been teaching seminars in Las Vegas using the craps table as his laboratory for psychokinesis. He has led groups where they focus on having the dice come up with certain numbers. This is an amazing book filled with fascinating stories about the different groups he's led over the years, as well as insights about meditation, creating your own reality, and using the energy of the heart to create the life you desire. This is a highly recommended and enjoyable read. I have not yet had the opportunity to take a workshop from Dr. Gallenberger in Las Vegas, but I would like to in the future.

Jiang, Jia. *Rejection Proof.* Harmony, 2015. Discusses the author's quest to receive many rejections when he asked for things, so that he became immune to anyone saying no. Very interesting book, shows the possibilities of just asking for things and pushing past your fears in doing so. Seems really scary to me which means he's probably onto something!

Kaplan, Janice and Marsh, Barnaby. *How Luck Happens: Using the New Science of Luck to Transform Life, Love, and Work.* Dutton, 2018. This book explores luck via the two authors' perspectives: Professor Barnaby Marsh who works at the Institute for Advanced Studies in Princeton, NJ, and his journalist friend, Janice Kaplan. They examine luck through various stories and anecdotes, as well as with the help of research from Professor Marsh's Luck Lab. They conclude that luck is a combination of chance, talent, and hard work, and that we have more control over it than we may realize.

An important concept in this book is the fact that chance AND luck can combine to create something powerful. The example they use is that you are going to fundraising dinner, and randomly sit next to an investor who funds the business idea you pitch to them. The chance part / random part is sitting next to this person. But the luck part, that you help drive, is you being ready to discuss your idea and sharing it with the investor. If you had just talked about sports or something random, you wouldn't have had this 'lucky' opportunity.

Larson, Cynthia Sue. *Quantum Jumps: An Extraordinary Science of Happiness and Prosperity.* Cynthia Larson Publisher, 2013.

Michel, Kevin L. *Moving Through Parallel Worlds to Achieve Your Dreams.* Kevin L. Michel, Publisher, 2013.

Muller, Thor and Becker, Lane. *Get Lucky: How To Put Planned Serendipity to Work For You And Your Business.* Jossey-

Bass, 2012. People make their own luck and so do organizations. They define serendipity as chance interacting with creativity. Allowing for serendipity within organizations can lead to innovations and great new product ideas.

Robbins, Anthony. *Awaken The Giant Within*. Simon & Schuster, 1992.

Robbins, Anthony. *Unlimited Power.* Nightengale-Conant, 1986.

Schoemaker, Paul J. H. "Forget Dumb Luck – Try Smart Luck: Strategies to Get Lady Luck on Your Side." MBR Spring 2021. Dr. Schoemaker describes a 4-part framework for accessing what he calls "Smart Luck." This article is filled with many important guidelines for improving your luck, emphasizing both business and personal aspects of luck. Each concept has two parts.

The framework is below. My comments on the framework are in *italics.*

1. Create Opportunities
a. Position yourself better
b. Improve peripheral vision
2. Assess Risks & Returns
a. Take Calculated Risks *Understand statistics and risk/reward tradeoffs.*
b. Adopt a Portfolio View *Keep the big picture in mind, don't lose focus on one single issue.*
3. Refine Your Strategy
a. More Shots on Goals *Try lots of things, many will fail but lots will succeed!*
b. Build Wider Networks *The more people you know and interact with the luckier you will be. We see this theme over and over from authors regarding luck.*
4. Change Your Attitude
a. Conquer Your Fears *Easier said than done!*
b. Make Your Own Luck *You can do it; this guidebook can help.*

Taylor, Sandra Anne. *Quantum Success: The Astounding Science of Wealth and Happiness.* Hay House, 2006.

Vernon, Michael (The Professor). *Do's and Don'ts of Dice.* You can find this on Michael's website at

https://playing4keeps.com/gambling-books/craps-book/. Michael taught various classes in Las Vegas and Taos for many years, and I was fortunate to have taken one of his seminars on craps in Las Vegas in the early 2000's. His main point was that there is energy present in the universe, and we can teach ourselves to be observant and aware of this energy in order to use it to improve our lives. He calls his approach for this applied metaphysics. His 'lab' was the craps tables of Las Vegas where he taught us to be aware of the energy and what was happening around us as we played, and we could see the outcomes of our 'awareness' instantly in the rolls of the dice. It was fun, and we did win some money! But applied metaphysics was the primary focus of the class. You can still get Michael's books on his website, though he has retired from doing in-person lessons and seminars.

Wiseman, Richard. *The Luck Factor.* Arrow Books, 2004. Dr. Wiseman has studied luck and people who consider themselves lucky for many decades. He is probably one of the foremost luck experts. A summary of his key principles is below:

1. Maximize Chance Opportunities

Lucky people are skilled at creating, noticing, and acting upon chance opportunities. They do this in several ways, including networking, adopting a relaxed attitude to life and by being open to new experiences.

2. Listen to Lucky Hunches

Lucky people make effective decisions by listening to their intuition and gut feelings. In addition, they take steps to actively boost their intuitive abilities by, for example, meditating and clearing their mind of other thoughts.

3. Expect Good Fortune

Lucky people are certain that the future is going to be full of good fortune. These expectations become self-fulfilling prophecies by helping lucky people persist in the face of failure and shape their interactions with others in a positive way.

4. Turn Bad Luck into Good

Lucky people employ various psychological techniques to cope with, and often even thrive upon, the ill fortune that comes their way. For example, they spontaneously imagine how things could have been worse, do not dwell on the ill fortune, and take control of the situation.

Zeland, Vadim. *Reality Transurfing Steps I-IV.* CreateSpace Independent Publishing Platform, 2016. This is a strange yet wonderful book. It has been translated to English from the original Russian by Joanna Dobson. It contains rather unique views on how our reality is constructed, and there are many gems throughout the book. One of my favorite quotes from the book is: If it works out, great! And if not, even better!

Trivedi, Nikhil Basu. *The Rise of The Solo Capitalists.*

https://nbt.substack.com/p/the-rise-of-the-solo-capitalists

Discusses one-person venture capital funds. Their networks and deep knowledge of a particular industry / niche can make this possible. Discusses implications for traditional venture capital firms and speculates that this will be a permanent feature of VC. An example of this would be Harry Stebbings who runs the 20 Minute VC podcast as well as has a fund. He says he operates at the intersection of venture capital

and media. Check out Harry's website at twentyminutevc.com.
This article relates to Chapter 3—Big Networks = Big Luck in
Get Luck Now!

Appendix 2

More Lucktivities

This appendix builds on the lucktivities laid out in the previous chapters. There is some overlap!

Exercise 1

What good luck have you had in your life already?

Take a few moments to think about all the events in your life that could be described as 'good luck.' This could be having someone go on a date with you that you were really interested in, getting a job, meeting someone really cool that became a great friend, really anything that you think could be good luck, probably was! Of course, good luck is usually accompanied by things like taking action, having a positive mindset, working hard, and all those types of things. But underneath, there can also be the element of good luck that you encouraged into your life by doing other things too. Write this in your journal or on your computer or however you take notes. Refer to this often and over time I bet that you will recall many lucky events that have happened to you!

Exercise 2

Checklist: Daily Habits of Luck

- Maintain an attitude of curiosity, open-mindedness, and acceptance.

- Ask yourself, in good times and challenging times: "What is great about this?" or if it is a really challenging time, "What COULD be great about this?"
- Believe the universe is working for you and conspiring to help you.
- Be on the lookout for Ambient Fortune at all times.
- Be open to universal invitations that may be strongly suggesting you do a particular thing to lead to great luck!
- Take a deep breath and be thankful for everyone in your life, your health and all the great things you have.

Exercise 3

World's Friendliest and Greatest Customer

A good friend of mine jokes that I am the friendliest customer when we go out to eat at a restaurant. I guess it is maybe true! I do enjoy being very kind and friendly to the waiters or waitresses because I find that it is a nice thing to do, and selfishly I feel like I always get better service if I do that. It turns into a self-fulfilling prophesy, and we get a good laugh out of it. You can easily incorporate that into your dining experience if you choose. And you could also do this with any service person or someone who is helping you with something—a cashier, store employee, really anyone you encounter. I think this will make your interactions much more fun and interesting!

I have a small anecdote about this: I was in the drive-thru lane at McDonald's recently in Florida. While I know it isn't the healthiest thing in the world, I was buying some burgers for my dad and stepmom for lunch (and for me!). I pulled up and put my order in, and I was very positive and said, "Thank you very much, I appreciate you!" as we signed off on the ordering speaker, and I drove around to pay. Now, I didn't really think too much of my world's friendliest customer approach, because I pretty much always do this, but as I went to the window to pay, the worker said to me "You know, you were so nice and polite that I'm going to use a promo code for you and take one of those burgers off the bill." Wow! I thought what an amazing and simple thing just being nice is, and it made me smile and say a big "Thank you!" And she was happy that I was happy, and it was a win-win. So, for such a small thing, and whether you actually get something of monetary value is beside the point because it was a nice little moment during the day. Try this!

This can also be applied to any situation where you are the customer—at the gym, the dry cleaners, the grocery store, drug store, etc. Wherever you interact with someone as the 'customer' and treating the employee and the whole situation in a friendly and happy way will make their day and even if it doesn't, you can still radiate happiness and joy to the world!

Exercise 4

Customer of the Month/Year/Decade

This is closely related to the previous exercise, so perhaps you can include it as part of your repertoire. Sometimes I imagine there is an award for 'customer of the year' at places I visit, and I am secretly hoping that there is a $1,000,000 prize for the nicest and best customer that comes to the establishment. I haven't won $1,000,000 yet, but you never know!

Also, in the past I've seen stories where someone is the 1,000,000th customer or something and there's a big party and event made out of that. Who knows? It could happen to you!

Exercise 5

Yes! This must be the free one!?

Sometimes when you are at the store and perhaps an item doesn't ring up correctly or there's a slight glitch, I will jokingly say "Ahh! This must be the free item?" Now you have to say this in a joking and funny way, or the cashier may not be as entertained as you are, but usually it gets a laugh out of them. Now is that going to bring luck to you? Maybe! I have yet to actually get a free item this way, but you never know! ☺

Exercise 6

Doing Something Nice for Someone Each Day

Here is a list of some super easy things that you can do for other people each day that can make others really happy and thankful, and make yourself feel good:

- If someone is behind you at the grocery store grabbing a cart, just pull one out for them and offer it to them. Easy!
- If you are shopping and see a shirt or something on the floor that can easily be picked up and hung back up, go ahead and do it! (I imagine maybe a hidden camera is waiting to reward a $500 shopping spree to me—not yet though!)

- Hold the door open for people even if they are a small distance away. Easy!
- Always let people that are walking in a parking lot go in front of you if you are driving.

Exercise 7

Park far away and enjoy the rain!

On a rainy day, if you have to go to the store or gym or whatever and you are driving, and it is raining, instead of lamenting that it is raining, change it up and celebrate the rain! I feel like this mindset shift can bring luck into your life. There's no scientific evidence whatsoever. Just my opinion! So how do you do this? Simple, just park far, grab your umbrella, and enjoy walking into your final stop. Bonus: Also can be done on non-rainy days. Observation: Does anyone carry or use an umbrella anymore? Seems like lately when I am using my umbrella, I am the only one and everyone else is just running through the rain. Maybe it is because I'm walking slowly and enjoying myself, I don't know...

Exercise 8

8 Lucktivities Specific to Ambient Fortune™ and Universal Invitations

1. Fortune Awareness Hour

Dedicate one hour each day to heightened awareness of Ambient Fortune. During this hour, consciously look for signs, coincidences, or opportunities that might be universal invitations. Keep a small notebook handy to jot down any observations or hunches. You could of course add this to your luck journal.

2. Serendipity Walks

Take a 15-minute walk in a new area each week with the intention of discovering Ambient Fortune. Be open to unexpected encounters, interesting sights, or overheard conversations. Consider any unusual occurrences as potential universal invitations.

3. Fortune Meditation

Practice a 10-minute daily meditation focusing on Ambient Fortune. Visualize yourself surrounded by a field of positive energy and opportunity. End the meditation by setting an intention to recognize universal invitations throughout your day.

4. Random Page Oracle

Once a week, randomly open a book and point to a passage. Reflect on how this message might be a universal invitation or relate to Ambient Fortune in your life. Look for ways to apply this "oracle" to your week ahead.

5. Ambient Fortune Journaling

Keep a daily journal dedicated to Ambient Fortune. Each evening, write down at least one instance where you noticed Ambient Fortune or received a universal invitation. Review your journal weekly to spot patterns or recurring themes.

6. Fortune Trigger Object

Choose a small object (like a coin or stone) to carry with you. Whenever you touch or see this object, use it as a reminder to tune into Ambient Fortune. Ask yourself, "What opportunity or invitation might be present in this moment?" Reflect on the outcomes and any unexpected benefits.

7. Fortune Sharing Circle

Form a small group (in-person or online) dedicated to discussing Ambient Fortune. Meet weekly to share experiences, universal invitations received, and insights gained. Collectively brainstorm ways to be more open to Ambient Fortune in daily life.

8. Fortune Reframe Practice

At the end of each day, choose one "negative" event that occurred. Challenge yourself to reframe it as a potential universal invitation or manifestation of Ambient Fortune. Write down three possible positive outcomes or lessons that could result from this event. See page 36 for Fortune Reframe *Detailed Steps*.

Appendix 3

Words to Live By

The following pages draw from the first letter of each of the words in the title of this book—Get Luck Now. For each letter, there is a dedicated page with a selection of words, and short descriptions of how those words and concepts relate to bringing luck into your life. There are different ways to use these lists. Below are a few suggestions.

- Pick one word from one of the letters that speaks to you. For example, you might pick the word Goals (using the G in Get). Then you could look at your goals, or create new ones, that would prompt you to look for more luck in your life, or however you wanted to interpret it.

- Three Word Pick: Take a word from any of the letters in Get, and in Luck, and in Now. For example, you might pick the word Energy (E from Get), the word Laughter (L from Luck), and the word Openness (from the O in Now). You could then see how many ways you could incorporate Energy, Laughter, and Openness into your quest for bringing luck into your life. You could do this for a specific day or for a whole week, etc.

- Randomly pick a couple letters from your first name and then find words that match these letters and try to incorporate those concepts into bringing yourself good luck.
- Really experiment as this is meant to be a fun way to think differently about luck and guide you to experience it in ways that, for you, may be out-of-the-ordinary.

Hopefully, this is a fun and creative way for you to think about luck in different ways. It can help keep things fresh for you by providing different words and ideas you can use to bring the awareness of good luck and fortune into your life.

Each letter—with words and descriptions of those concepts—begins on the next page.

Get Luck Now Words to Live By: G

Grow Have a growth mindset to increase chances of lucky opportunities.

Gratitude Appreciating what you have can attract more positive experiences.

Grit Persistence in the face of challenges often leads to lucky breakthroughs.

Goals Clear objectives can help guide you to fortunate circumstances.

Generosity Giving to others often results in unexpected rewards.

Genius Tapping into your unique talents can create lucky breaks.

Grace Moving through life with ease and poise attracts good fortune.

Gumption Initiative and resourcefulness often lead to lucky outcomes. Ask for what you want! The world may give it to you.

Get Luck Now Words to Live By: E

Explore Venturing into new territories increases chances for lucky discoveries.

Engage Active participation in life creates more opportunities for luck.

Embrace Accepting change and challenges can lead to fortunate outcomes.

Energy High vitality attracts positive circumstances and people.

Enthusiasm Passion and excitement draw lucky opportunities closer.

Empathy Understanding others can lead to unexpected beneficial connections.

Empower Feeling capable and confident attracts lucky breaks.

Experiment Trying new things increases the likelihood of stumbling upon good fortune.

Get Luck Now Words to Live By: T

Trust Believe in your ability to create luck.

Transform Changing yourself and your circumstances can lead to lucky outcomes.

Timing Recognizing and seizing the right moment is key to creating luck. The timing of the universal invitation!

Tenacity Persistence in the face of setbacks can lead to lucky breakthroughs. The harder you work the luckier you get.

Thrive Flourishing in your environment attracts positive opportunities.

Thoughts Make it a priority to have positive thoughts and minimize or eliminate negative thoughts so that you can manifest lucky situations.

Transcend Rising above limitations can create unexpected fortunate outcomes.

Get Luck Now Words to Live By: L

Leverage Using your resources wisely can create lucky opportunities.

Listen Being attentive to others and your environment can reveal fortunate paths.

Learn Acquiring new knowledge often leads to lucky discoveries.

Leap Taking bold, calculated risks can result in fortunate outcomes.

Love Opening your heart can lead to unexpected lucky connections.

Lead Taking initiative often puts you in the path of good fortune.

Legacy Building something lasting can create lucky opportunities for others.

Laughter A positive, joyful attitude often attracts lucky circumstances.

Get Luck Now Words to Live By: U

Uncover Keep your eyes and ears ready to discover luck and hidden possibilities.

Understand Deep comprehension can reveal lucky possibilities.

Unleash Releasing your full potential often results in lucky breaks.

Uplift Elevate others and yourself to attract positive circumstances.

Unity Bonding with others can create lucky synergies.

Unique Embracing and celebrating your individuality can lead to fortunate distinctions. This also applies to events, trips, jobs, etc. Unique and unusual things are to be valued.

Unwind Relaxation and stress relief can open you up to lucky opportunities and let you see the ambient fortune present.

Get Luck Now Words to Live By: C

Courage Bravery in the face of uncertainty often leads to lucky outcomes.

Curiosity An inquisitive nature can uncover fortunate discoveries.

Create Bringing new ideas to life can generate lucky opportunities.

Connect Building relationships often results in serendipitous encounters.

Consistent Regular positive habits can accumulate into lucky circumstances.

Compassion Kindness towards others can return as unexpected good fortune.

Collaborate Working with others can multiply chances for lucky breaks.

Celebrate Acknowledging successes can attract more positive outcomes.

Get Luck Now Words to Live By: K

Karma Positive actions you take often return as fortunate circumstances in your life.

Kindness Generosity of spirit can lead to unexpected lucky outcomes.

Knowledge Information and wisdom can guide you towards fortunate decisions.

Keen Sharp awareness can help you spot and seize lucky opportunities.

Kick-start Initiating projects or ideas can set lucky events in motion.

Knuckles I put a random word here to see if anyone read this far. Tell me if you did.

Knack Natural talents, when developed, can lead to fortunate specializations.

Get Luck Now Words to Live By: N

Navigate Skillfully steering through life's challenges can lead to lucky outcomes.

Nurture Caring for yourself and others can create a fertile ground for good fortune.

Network Building connections can increase chances for lucky encounters.

Nourish Feeding your mind, body, and soul can attract positive circumstances.

Notion Entertaining new ideas can lead to fortunate innovations.

Novelty Embracing the new & different can result in lucky discoveries. See lucktivities of spontaneity day, micro-adventures and becoming yes man or woman.

Nobility Acting with honor and integrity can attract respect and fortunate opportunities.

Get Luck Now Words to Live By: O

Observe Always be looking around and taking note of your surroundings because there could be a lucky break / ambient fortune waiting to be discovered!

Optimize Improving processes and systems can create lucky efficiencies.

Opportunity Recognizing and seizing chances can lead to fortunate outcomes; remember that ambient fortune is always present.

Openness Being receptive to new ideas and experiences can invite lucky encounters.

Originality Unique approaches can lead to unexpected fortunate results. Being yourself is something that is natural to you and there are people out there who will love you for it!

Oasis Creating a positive space in your life can attract lucky circumstances. Having a relaxing playlist or YouTube video to watch can help.

Outlook A positive perspective can help you recognize and create good fortune. Welcoming the good things in life can be your default mode if you choose it!

Get Luck Now Words to Live By: W

Wonder Cultivate an appreciation for the possibilities of luck; a sense of awe and curiosity can open you up to magical lucky moments.

Wisdom Accumulated life knowledge can guide you towards fortunate decisions.

Wealth Abundance in various forms can create lucky opportunities. Wealth can be many things besides monetary: relationships, health, gratitude.

Wellbeing Good health—mental, physical, spiritual—can position you for fortunate circumstances. You must be healthy to capitalize on good luck.

Willpower Strong determination can help you create your own luck.

Wholeness Feeling complete and integrated can attract positive outcomes.

Worthiness Believing in your own value can draw lucky opportunities to you. You are enough and are amazing!

Wow Cultivating a sense of amazement can help you attract good fortune.

Appendix 4

Phone Picture Checklist

Take a picture of this page and keep it handy in your smartphone so you can refer back to it when going into a situation, meeting, event, etc. that you want to make sure you are ready to see and find the ambient fortune that is there, waiting for you. It is formatted to fit the screen of most smartphones, and you can always adjust it a bit for your screen. Enjoy! Permission is granted to photograph this page only for personal use.

Mindset
Openminded, Aware, Curious, Grateful, Expecting
 Greatness and Excellence.

Attitude
Action-oriented, friendly, and outgoing, embracing
differences that make life exciting.

Principles
1. Spot Ambient Fortune™ everywhere.
2. Heed universal invitations calling you to
   experience good luck.
3. Unlock good luck through action.

Questions to ask yourself
What is right or great about this?
What could be even better?
Why am I so consistently lucky?
Why does good luck happen to me so often?
Where is the ambient fortune here?
What universal invitation is calling to me?

Remember
Taking action is the key to unlocking the Ambient
Fortune™ that surrounds you. Stay open, take
initiative, and watch as luck flows into your life!

About the Author

Bill James grew up in Rockford, IL and graduated from the University of Notre Dame with a degree in Finance. He has worked in real estate, as a trust and investment officer for a bank, and for almost 20 years as an Investment Director and Risk Manager at the University of Notre Dame Investment Office. He has advised family offices on portfolio construction, and hedge fund and private equity allocations. He currently serves as an investment committee member and advisor for a health care system in Indiana. He has a deep interest in trend following trading systems, as well as in psychology and human behavior. Get Luck Now! is his first book.

Learn more at www.getlucknow.com

www.ingramcontent.com/pod-product-compliance
Lightning Source LLC
Chambersburg PA
CBHW051430090426
42737CB00014B/2903